After The Blooming

After The Blooming

H-K MEYER

安

A REFRACTIONS PAPERBACK ORIGINAL

ISBN: 979-8-9934772-0-6

First Edition: 2025

安 Refractions Publishing.

CONTENTS

Epilogue

I. Incantation

II. Interrogation

III. Elegy

for the ones who dared

After The Blooming

Epilogue

Not river, not wire
just the branch's breath
before the fire.
Not you, not me,
just the door
we couldn't close.

I.   INCANTATION

Entry

You move me to walk
the jagged edges of your kisses,
to swim channels of lust
hidden in the heart of prudence.

The way your thumb traced my hip,
a question that needed no answer,
until I was a tunnel of rhythmic orgasms,
the orchid bursting to
the wild tango of a loud silence.

You move me
into a language
without consonants.

After The Blooming

(For the gardener of lilies and other holy
disturbances)

You kneel,
not to pray, but to split the earth
with your bare hands,
planting verbs where roots should be.

The soil remembers your name,
whispers it to the worms
in a language of almost
and not yet.

I watch from the hedges,
a shadow stitched from old manuals,
learning hunger from the way
you curse the weeds
but spare the thistles.

At dusk, you unspool the hose,
water unfurling like a question
neither of us can answer.
The lilies nod, drunk
on this silent catechism,
while I, ever the student,
count the syllables of your spine
bending toward the light.

Flow

When you're gone,
it's not your eyes I reach for,
but the hush between your sighs,
the strength of your calves,
where the story of us
first found breath.

When your world frays,
I sit at your altar,
your feet in my hands,
oil warming in a bowl,
my fingers rewriting
your sorrow.

And that is when
your quiet
restores me.

With or Without

The morning sun forgets its fury
until you leave.
Then its light lingers,
a gold coin left in my palm
by a passing stranger.

Dew wears jasmine's perfume
where your footsteps last paused.
In your absence,
it beads on the grass,
each drop a lens
remembering your gaze.

The breeze, penitent,
carries the scent of turned soil
then stills, as if listening
for the echo of your laugh
caught in the chimes.

With you:
the world is a chapel.
Without you:
the sanctuary holds only
this quiet,
this patient tending
of the light you left behind.

Sunday Revelations

My heaven is the look in your eyes
just after we kiss,
the pause before the world resumes.

My heaven is birdsong
threading the ridgeline,
its breath carving the horizon.

My heaven is holding you,
your breath softened
by the weight of everything unsaid.

My heaven is Queen Anne's Lace,
not called, only noticed.

My heaven is the grace
in the valleys of your body,
how it carries
what I never managed to.

My heaven is the scent of soil
before rain,
and even more
just after.

My heaven is your quiet,
the way it opens
under my mouth
like it was always meant to.

My heaven is a dog
offering trust
without proof.

And Sunday,
writing
while the morning
remembers me.

Allegro in A Minor

You move me
not as object, but as origin.
Your breath chisels verses into flesh
and even light
arches its back at your command.

Your kiss tastes like scripture
written in the wet vowels of desire.
Your restraint
only heightens the hunger,
like a locked door that moans
in its longing to be trespassed.

I bloom in your orbit,
a magnolia unashamed,
petals slick with thunder,
drunk on the choreography
of our unsaid,
our undone,
our becoming.

You move me
not forward
but inward
where I unravel
just to be read again.

What the Light Forgot

You say misremember
like memory isn't just
another kind of hunger.

I watched you pretend
not to notice
my noticing.

Call it eclipse if you must,
but we both know
darkness requires collusion.

What you called clarity,
I called learning to breathe fire
without burning down
the house you built
out of certainty.

As for the tropics,
you're right.
I never earned them.

But you
never earned
the right to call their burning
closure
while the embers
still spelled my name
in your handwriting.

Light moves on.
But it leaves behind
the stubborn stains
of what it once illuminated.

Look closer:
even your transparency
casts shadows.

II. INTERROGATION

Reach

I reach for you
not like night for day,
but like the pause
before their meeting
where neither is whole.

Not to hold,
not to follow
only to remain
just near enough
to shadow
what I can't touch
and won't forget.

Where Touch Remembers

It aches
not where sin festers,
but when touch sings.

Where your moan
becomes a hymn
and climax tastes
like consecration.

Here, piety is exile,
and in its absence,
we worship.

And the ache,
the holy ache
is where your body remembers
every forbidden gospel
written on the inside of your thighs.

Here,
I do not worship you.
I dissolve.

And in that dissolution,
love
becomes
a rebellion.

After Neruda

Tonight, I could write
the truest lines:
the moon withdrawn,
the wind unsure of its name.

We made love,
and I needed to leave.
Through nights like this one,
she watched me vanish
between her exhales.

She fed me
with bread and wine.
She took me
between her knees,
blessing the dark.

Tonight, I could write
what I dare not send:
she is burdened,
and I cannot lift it.

Still,
I long for the echo
left in her sheets.

I will find her
in songs with no chorus.
I will whisper
monastic cravings
in the scent of pine
where her voice once lived.

Tonight, I could write
not the saddest lines,
but the clearest ones.

And the glass of rum
still warm
remembers both our songs.

Of the Broken

I am of the broken
and yet cannot be broken:
a mangrove rooted
in tidal blood,
consecrating dirt
into sacrament.

Behind me:
sanctity's ribs bend
above the waterline,
innocence split
like a pomegranate
left too long
in God's blind spot.

(This is my birthright:
to dismantle the pyre
with the same hands
that light candles,
to graft pause
onto the psalmist's
missing page.)

I am of the broken
but salvage what sinks:
the hymnal's waterlogged spine,
the crucifix
still warm
from the heretic's grip.

Hope?
A tendon straining
against the tide's
retraction.

And still, I walk.
Knowing you
might just be there
to keep me
unbroken.

Heretic's Hymn

Let us burn nothing.
Let the fear stand
a rotted shrine
we no longer kneel to.

Let the chalk lines
we drew fade.
Let the walls
we raised
learn to tremble
without our hands.

Let the commandments
crumble like yesterday.
Let the sacred
they guarded
become a psalm
for the faithless.

Let me be the heretic
who lights no fire,
who only watches
as the old gods
turn to dust
and call it rain.

In Conversation

A flip of the hair
to wipe away transgressions.

A flick of the wrist
to discard assumptions.

A pinch of the nostrils
to shutter presumptions.

A tug of the earlobe
to divert opinions.

A clearing of the throat
to submerge rumors.

A twist of the tongue
not to evade,
but to finally say:
I wanted to love you
and couldn't.

Sleight of Hand

The wheel spun
as it always had
a quiet blasphemy
against stillness,
as if certain
we'd never demand
its fate.

Then: a stutter.
The hitch of a loom
when the thread snaps.
My ribs:
an empty shuttle
clattering to the floor.

I stepped off.
Not in defiance,
but like a word
finally spoken
after years
of choking on its shape.

You stood
where the path forked,
facing the direction
we'd called not yet.

Behind us,
the wheel unravels
into a thousand threads,
each one a path
we could have taken.

Ahead,
only the wind
braiding our shadows
into something
that doesn't need
a center.

Lost Thread

I began a poem about you
but it wouldn't come.

Not like before,
when your gaze
offered distance
I believed was home.

When the crook of my neck
was your morning refuge,
and lull
didn't feel like proof
of aching.

Now,
your face
refuses my page.

And even spring
can't finish the line
you left me in.

What Gathers in Absence

Is it the way your pulse leapt
across the patio
on a boat of tears
that first night we kissed?

Is it simply the fracture
of your smile, lips parting
rising slightly into
a scripture I couldn't translate?

Is it how your hand slowly
slides across your stomach,
tracing a path through my follies
I ache to follow?

Is it the rhythm of your walk
or the rhyme of your hips?
Sublime, it sways onlookers
to repent in its wake?

Is that why I gorge on your laughter,
then starve
tonguing the void
for the carcass of your voice?

Letters Folded in Salt

I saw you in the stillness
before the monsoon gathered,
where the sky
unclenches its fist
a moment too late.

You had your back to the wind,
but your heart faced me.
Even then,
you moved like grief
practicing its exit.

The mango leaf
it wasn't a sign.
It slipped,
one more green syllable
added to the earth's
unfinished sentence.

The magpies were watching.
They do not mourn.
They inscribe.
Their cries are not sorrow,
they are the ledger's
unblinking ink.

I've kept your scent
in a bone-lipped jar,
between the cinnamon
and the gunpowder,
where the vanished go
to be tasted
but never consumed.

Yes.
I am the tide,
but I never chose
the pull.
I only wanted
to be the echo
that outlives
the voice.

The Subject Replies

I was the still
before your prayer,
the pause that asked
too much of breath.

I moved so the silence
would have something to echo,
so the light might stain you
in places you hid.

You mistook mercy for offering,
and my reserve for need.
But I was already naming your hunger
aloud, alone, alive.

What you swallowed
I sang.

III. ELEGY

Thieves

We stole moments,
a glance among the worshippers,
smiles glinting off
pints of golden cider,
our thoughts threading through
the static of drunk conversations.

We stole discretion,
contacts traded like relics
beneath antique lights and trees
with bark like old regrets,
thick, dark, slow to surrender.

We stole hope,
in your bed, breathing
lavender, basil, rosemary.
We tossed away strawbales
of fatalism,
our hearts wishing to
no longer ferry
what could not be tamed,
our remaining years
not so numerous.

We stole passion,
moving from room to room,
hotels with thread-counted grace,
quilts in cold cabins
learning our dance
by the heat we left behind.

And what of destiny?
Are we its dandelions,
soft, unnoticed,
pregnant with healing and magic,
carried by the whims of the lost,
and yet, still windward,
still ready to bloom
in someone else's unknowing?

The Sweet of You

I was mesmerized
not by the ocean's lull,
but by your eyes,
quiet as dusk,
offering shelter
without price.

They held my joy
like it was theirs to keep,
absorbed my guilt
without flinching,
a language of mercy
spoken in glances.

We lay on the couch,
a low, orbiting capsule:
touched like lovers,
spoke like friends
too wise to lie,
too late to begin again.

You were sweet.
Not soft,
not sugar,
but the sweetness
of a fig split open,
its flesh glistening
with the patience
of trees.

The feather paused.
Not falling,
not flight,
just long enough
to let me memorize
the stillness
between our breaths.

Take Good Care

You sat on the steps,
elbows on knees,
your face hidden,
a question you no longer wanted
answered.

I came through the folding doors
with bags that leaned me off-center
and a smile too wide
to mean welcome.

I wanted to reach for you.
Not to apologize,
but to see if your body
would still flinch or soften.

You wore a new sundress,
new hair,
a body carved by time
and something unsaid.

But your heart,
I knew its rhythm.
It used to lift
when I said the right thing.

You touched my arm.
Not affection,
not dismissal.

Outside, our smiles
tried the same lock
with different keys.

I told myself
the air would sort it out.

We loaded the trunk
with everything we didn't say.

The dog's tail
lifted like a question
we weren't ready to ask.

You said you missed me.
Your eyes didn't wait.

We kissed.
You smiled.
You drove.

I stayed.

Reflex

I found myself
reaching for you last night.
My right hand searching
for the safety
of your left breast.

The bed said nothing.
But the space
where you once breathed
was still warm
with refusal.

Trace

I knew
you would reach.

Not out of longing,
but from the reflex
of the body
remembering safety
as absence.

I did not move.
I wanted to.
But the air between us
needed
to keep its shape.

And you.
You always did
sleep deeper
than goodbye.

Tango for the Unnamed

I know your gait,
not your name.
A slow tango,
hips swaying
like a bridge
over water
that refuses
to hold still.

Dawn offers coffee.
Your wrist tilts
a feathered pulse
against the cup's rim.
I memorize the heat
left behind.

Now I know your name.
Now I know my fate:
to wander the corridor
where our shadows
never quite
touched.

The Bread You Bake

the bread you bake
the art you flay
the love you break
fills me
with light
with claws
with flight
dares me
to bow
to gnaw
to blaspheme.

And the care you give
the days you live
make me grieve
time's
relentless
sugaring
of the bone.

And Yet...

Rain teases the soil.
Still, butterflies flutter
over marguerite and marigold,
eggplants clutch their green pulse,
peapods stretch toward becoming.

Under bruised sky,
leaves beg for a sliver of sun.
Papaya and maracuya bow
at the feet of light,
obedient in their ache
for the balance once promised.

Petrichor rises like an offering.
Chameleons cut through wet growth,
color betraying nothing.
Toloks lumber backward,
their tails armored
in mourning-black rings.

And still,
with espresso in hand,
I sit in the stillness
blind to
the symmetry around me.

Raindrops descend
in careful geometry.
What remains of you
does not.

What We Failed to Say

We burned the first draft.
The paper curled like a map
of a country that never was;
its borders drawn in phosphorus,
its legends reduced to scent.

Now the poem is gone,
but the tree still falls
in the white space between
your stop and my go.

The sparrows, pragmatic,
snatch carbon from the air,
weaving nests from the remains
of what we failed to say.

Sparrows weave nests from calm.
Jasmine opens anyway.

Even the ashes rhyme.
Even the silence, now,
is a kind of song.

Water Runs Through It

She draws the bath
in a bowl of split oranges,
their skins collapsing
like surrendered prayers.

Steam fogs the mirror.
She does not look.
Drinks from a chipped glass
where the ice
has outlived
its purpose.

Barefoot, she rides the seam
between today and yesterday.
A room still echoing
what the drums
refuse to hear.

Frogs sing beneath the sill.
A butterfly pauses
on the faucet's lip,
its wings folding
like two pale letters
never sent.

She lowers herself
into air,
into citrus and heat,
into the shape
of beginning
without the weight
of a name.

Margins

I thought I stopped
writing you.
Still the ink
runs its own regress.

Not to your name,
but the white space
around it,
where my hands
never
quite
landed.

The hinge creaks.
The door stays shut.
The silence,
finally,
is mine.

Notes

"After Neruda" was inspired by Pablo Neruda's
"Tonight, I Can Write (The Saddest Lines)" and follows
its cadence and structure.

"Of The Broken" was inspired by my grandmothers:
Astrelle and Andrea

Acknowledgments

Johan and Nigel, for continuing to teach and inspire an old man.

J. Luna for her kindness and patience.

Gratitude to my mother for her resolve and to Natacha, my sister, for her smile.

And…to my father who fed me with books.

www.ingramcontent.com/pod-product-compliance
Lightning Source LLC
Chambersburg PA
CBHW051434090426
42737CB00014B/2964